A Collection Ot verse

By

Alistair Muir B.A.(Hons)

Soul Ascendant

for Maureen

Two souls yet just one body here
and as you leave I shed a tear.
For you were soulmate, lover, friend,
a person on whom I'd depend.
To steer me on a course that's fair,
despite not being as a pair.
But on our own yet sharing souls,
with all the love that it extols.
And now I have to say farewell,
to part of me I know so well.
Your soul and mine now part for good,
upon this Earth but fate yet could
unite us in the other place.
The one of peace and calm and grace.
To where your soul ascends to be,
a second chance with liberty.
I watch it rise, diaphanous,
the colours bright and sensuous.
And as it goes it starts to rain,
then it begins. The awful pain.
Of separation, loss and ire,
I feel at odds with God, on fire.
How cruel is fate upon this day,
my grief a picture on display.

Alistair Muir 2017

The Birds

Birds fly across the rising sun,
bring fear to every mother's son.
For they are fragile and untried,
come from a land we all deride.
A place of lies and total fear,
no freedom for the people here.
Like mushrooms they are in the dark,
locked up for any crass remark.
And fed the bullshit of the state,
no need for them to remonstrate.
These active sponges soak up lies,
and kept in check by loyal spies.
But we look on and fear the crown,
the leader who likes to look down
upon his minions blind and true.
It is a lofty creaking view.
For truth will out in time, with fate,
and he held guilty for the State.
No liberty or freedom for
dissenters, those who know the score.
Yet till that time like Hitchcock fans
we fear the birds, arrests and bans.
But most of all the brinkmanship
the need to fight and brandish whip.
Take on the might of U.S. pride,
a dangerous and fruitless ride.
For Donald is no different,
he hates a challenge or dissent.
And so the world just holds its breath,
while watching birds and fearing death.
For now they're kept within their nests,
while North Korea runs its tests.
Preparing to let loose the kind,
the homing sort not flying blind.
But to a target pre-conceived,
to where they will be ill-received.
Thus Armageddon is so near
the path is open, very clear.

3

And in that place the people wait,
are told the war's commensurate.
With U.S. need to spread its wings,
the Devil drives and Donald sings.
Let's pray the birds fly not today,
let's sit in silence, hope and pray.
While all Koreans just obey,
their leader to the end of day.

Alistair Muir 2017

Hero

It felt so good the uniform,
way back, those days of Desert Storm.
The gun did talk and spit its rage,
and politicians likewise sage,
in Parliament did froth and seethe.
Exhorted war they did bequeath
on those who dared to question us.
The conflict would be glorious.
And so you joined as many had,
to tread the sands toward Baghdad.
But taking life became so hard,
the mem'ries you could not discard.
And then that fateful day arrived,
that caused such pain. Made you decide.
To drop the gun, pick up a pen,
a tool of peace, of calm, of Zen,
You wrote about the girl you saw,
an innocent they branded "whore".
A terrorist who should be dead,
sang they on propaganda fed.
The folks back home saw you as brave,
about the deed did sing and rave.
But it was you who shot the girl,
your mind unhinged and in a whirl.
You watched with horror red blood drain,
upon the white flag steep and stain.
Had she meant then to issue harm,
the flag she bore screamed only calm.
A sign of peace, she was not armed,
she should have been untouched, unharmed.
But friends and comrades rallied round
decrying logic, venting sound.
Of fury, lust to shoot not wait,
for death was his who'd hesitate.
They said you were a hero guy,
one people named their babies by.
But not to you so dark, depressed,
who left the force so broken, stressed.

The trauma understood by none,
the ones back home who saw it fun.
Who played their X-Box with desire,
to issue death with fearsome fire.
For them the war was just a game,
the likes of you were not to blame.
Yet it had been your finger, tense,
upon the trigger, your defence.
That had dispatched this girl that day,
for you no hero on display.
And so you sit in hospital,
rely on help more clinical.
To rationale the death of she
who only wanted liberty.

Alistair Muir 2017

The Night Urges

The cravings came in force last night,
with stealth and zeal they stole the light.
And into darkness were you cast,
a victim lashed upon the mast.
Your ship had into waters sailed,
where sailors chewed their lips and wailed.
For this was evil of a kind
that did attack and poison mind.
Made sane men weep for sanity,
while issuing profanity.
As God was not there to assist
the urges that did now persist.
They started off as just a spark,
a thought of something bleak and stark.
The drink you wanted to consume,
and take you to a place of doom.
That awful land where thirst was king,
and drinking was the only thing
that kept you going through the day.
And in the night kept fear at bay.
This spark erupted into fire
and stimulated your desire.
You balled your fists and tears rained down,
plunged now into a world of brown.
Of effluent in which you stood,
immobile as if made of wood.
And let the darkness have its way,
to take the colour leaving grey
your fragile mind. It felt so right,
and took you to a brand new height.

Now floating up amid a cloud,
you screamed for peace with fervour, loud.
Just thirty minutes had elapsed,
but on the floor you had collapsed.
The wave of need, the urge to drink
began to wane, to slip and sink.
Into your consciousness and hide,
returned to Hell as Satan's bride.
It left you weak but undeterred,
had come the call but you'd not heard.
For abstinence is life to you,
not dreaming in a world of glue.
Where time means nothing and you laze,
too frightened to address the days.
Now clean and dry comes self-esteem,
reality not just a dream.
And self-respect does sing and shout,
you cast your mask and costume out.
To be yourself, no drugs of choice,
your inner self has found a voice.
So now prepared for evil's urge,
you're ready to dispel and purge
the feelings from your tortured mind.
Just thirty minutes have to find
a place to meet, confront the beast.
Who would upon you dine and feast.
And you will find salvation too,
to live your life with pride anew.

Alistair Muir 2017

Fare Thee Well

So silence grips assembled friends,
as inner darkness here descends.
For we do love and hold a bond,
from which our friend does here abscond.
His life was shared with she who grieves,
amongst us now but who believes.
That he is in a better place,
yet here of irony's a trace.
For she would have him back right now,
if only God would so allow.
Here taken far to soon it seems,
to only now be seen in dreams.
This man will so be missed by all,
but he has heard the higher call.
Of God for it makes sense of this,
not some mistake, something remiss.
And as the rain falls on their heads,
the here departed severs threads.
But love will keep him in our hearts,
and memories where desire imparts.
Upon our minds and brings again,
this man to life without the pain.
Of separation, loss and hence
a gaping hole, no recompense.
Just happy thoughts of him will be
forever in our minds to see.
So fare thee well O friend of ours,
may you be with us all the hours.

Alistair Muir 2017

Glissando

Glissando comes and then she takes the stage,
a waif she looks yet muscular and fine.
Androgynous of shape she is new-age,
and all confess her dancing is divine.
A Russian queen of artistry and form,
her movement and deportment charm the eye.
Such modern dance does not in truth conform,
to classic moves yet wondrous none deny.

Glissando mellows hearts, unites them all,
where East meets West in unison of thought.
Here bonded by a dancer svelte and tall,
and all are joyous in the moment caught.
No politics can so create assent,
as this young maid from Heaven gladly sent.

Alistair Muir 2017

Thoughts of 1984

So cold the shivers stay your hand,
the temperature you cannot stand.
No gas for heating, nothing strange,
conditions set to now derange
your mind beleaguered by the State.
Perhaps it is commensurate
with mental torture. Would be right,
they haven't got the guts to fight.

At least electric have you still,
a light to see you type your fill.
A just reply to Tory shit,
this government who bit by bit
enforce the boot, the whip, and chain.
They do not hear us shout, explain
that PIP and Uni Credit stinks.
No matter what their expert thinks.

It leads to poverty and hate,
the need to riot, demonstrate.
Your tummy grumbles empty, since
you can't afford potatoes, mince.
Or anything that's fresh these days,
you feed yourself in different ways.
Make cheap bread last until it's green,
then toast it though it looks obscene.

How long before we take the streets,
autocracy objection meets.
Like those in France we will uprise,
our faces masked in some disguise.
Hurl molotovs and bricks and stones,
to immolate and shatter bones.
For we are tired of all their crap,
have fallen in the weasel's trap.

The empty words that mean suppress,
a wolf wrapped up in fancy-dress.

11

The working class attacked again,
the unemployed embraced by pain.
You shout unheard above the din,
let dialogue again begin.
But no, intransigent these twats,
parading in their deep blue hats.

Would have you firmly under foot,
all ruing that bold x you put
upon the ballot paper pure.
As Labour had seemed insecure,
their leadership at odds with all,
you wished you had heard Corbyn's call.
So now you curse Theresa May,
you live in hope that in the grey

some colour will arise and lead.
And listen to the poor who plead.
You pause to take a sip of tea,
no sugar, milk a fantasy.
And wonder how long will it be,
before your poems cease to be.
Withdrawn for rules of treason say,
remember Stalin, Hitler's way.

Just burn dissent and shoot them all
who shout against the Party's call.
A knock of door amid the night,
a blink and then you're out of sight.
A tired old mem'ry read by those
who stick two fingers up the nose
of Fascists called Conservatives.
Oppression rules, it feeds, it lives.

You look upon the shelf and find
a book you love and must re-bind.
It's Orwell's 1984,
a bible to so many score,
who see the way we go so clear.
It fills them with a sense of fear.

How many Winston's are there now,
and how long will we just allow

Big Brother to watch over us?
A nanny state insidious.
A glorified repressive state,
but no-one brave to designate
the rulers as the right-wing hell
we fought before with bullet, shell.
For this time they do rule so wise,
their government wrapped in disguise

as thinking, caring, good for all.
As Nazis did in thirties call.
What next for us this little isle?
Some Lebensraum? No, not our style.
We'll wait and watch the others fight,
join in with glee the side that's right.
In other words who Donald hates,
let's tick off all the left-wing States.

Before you know the birds will fly
and many millions left to die.
The only ones to then survive,
the bunkered swine who duck and dive.
And lick the boots of those who lead,
prepared to follow and to plead
allegiance to a right-wing mob,
so in cahoots with Trump the blob.

How did you see that all from this?
A frozen room and tea like piss?
You know not but it chills your bones,
discussing both these right-wing thrones.
How many others think this way?
To carry on and just obey?
Well fuck it all while you still can,
before the Press receives a ban.

You'll keep on writing, warning folk

that this is not some stupid joke.
Already they've arrested those,
for left-wing art, offensive prose.
A crowbar in our freedom's door,
then follows boot and Nazi whore.
A danger we must now abhor,
while we are crushed and on the floor.

You stop and huddle in the cold,
amazed at words so bleak and bold.
But reading them you feel so sure,
that fate is knocking at our door.

Alistair Muir 2017.

'Tis Halloween

'Tis Halloween and ghosts are out,
while demons, sprites and monsters scout.
For those who are so near to death,
to there inhale their final breath.
Condemn them to the darker side,
where just the cursed and damned reside.

Who with their last gave up their soul,
and now wait for the bell to toll.
Upon which time they meet the ghoul,
the Ferryman, a frightening tool
of Satan or the Prince of Lies.
Surrounded by a swarm of flies.

For he is wretched, putrid, rank,
who on the Styx which heaved and stank.
Did carry souls upon his sloop,
upon this river thick as soup.
Contaminated with remains,
the blood, the hearts, discarded brains.

A fetid stench that hangs in air,
an ambiance of great despair.
Transported cross this dreadful flow,
the dead feel dread begin to grow.
The land beyond is harsh and dry,
the fires erupt and vultures fly.

To pick at flesh and eyes of those
too slow, too tired or adipose.

Who fall, are left untended, lost,
their bones across the desert tossed.
This march which lasts a thousand nights,
the marchers sickened by the sights.

Of tortured things, the wand'ring blind,
who search in vain their souls to find.
So on and on the journey trails,
the frightening sound of screams and wails
rise up from pits along the road.
Some watch the bodies heave, explode.

And at the end they meet the One,
who holds their fate, the fallen Son.
His very gaze could melt the heart,
and so they feel its heat impart.
The flesh turns black and cooks like meat,
upon a grill as He does greet

his frightened flock. Resentful fools
whose skin melts now into the pools
of sweat and tears. The screaming hurts
as cross the floor their blood now spurts.
And each feels now the end of days,
in many sad and diff'rent ways.

Some flogged until the bones remain,
unthinkable and searing pain.
Some immolate in but a flash,
much better that than face the lash.
While others writhe in pain for hours,
as he takes souls, with greed devours.

But worst of all there is the Pit,
a seething mass of mulch and shit.
Where those unfortunates just burn,

unrighteous fools who rightly earn
this awful torture. There for years
as flesh dissolves and muscle sears.

The real Hell not mask and dress
you hire from shops to shock, impress
your fellow friends on Halloween.
This is a place you've never seen.
But should you falter, fall from grace,
detritus of the Human Race.

Then this is where you'll visit soon,
in morning, night or afternoon.
It matters not for here is night,
with hellish fire to issue light.
The Hell of myth and legend, real.
Make sure your breath they do not steal.

Alistair Muir 2017

Graveyard Rendezvous

It had been years since you'd been there,
now overgrown where once was bare.
The graveyard walls were thick and green,
with moss and vines, it looked obscene.
You had to force the gate, it stuck,
an omen then, some awful luck.
Indeed you felt uneasy, sick,
enhanced by fog confining, thick.

And in the gloom you strained to find,
the stones and statues, working blind.
You felt your way, you could not see,
but eyes adapted gradually.
Then through the gloom did stones appear,
and statues to the dead and dear.
And even here the weeds were rife,
insidious and evil life.

The words on tombstones such a loss,
now hidden 'neath a mass of moss.
A pale illumination glowed,
an eeriness the moon bestowed
upon the scene. A spectral sight.
The only source of any light.
No stars appeared through clouds so grey,
as if they had been scared away.

You found the grave eventually,
the last place where you hoped to be.
Invader of all peace and calm,
you feared a punishment or harm.
And with that thought you heard a crack,

a sound of some surprise attack.
But no just wildlife not some ghoul,
you laughed aloud, felt such a fool.

Then in the murk a statue saw,
not one that you had seen before.
It glowed with light, some trick of eye,
but then it moved and seemed to fly
across the ground. It floated, soared.
You fell to knees and prayed, implored
your God to right this trick of light.
For it was true an evil sight.

On op'ning eyes the statue stood,
upon the turf just like it should.
Examining the stony face,
you realised there was a trace
of mother in this work of art.
Her face and gait, it made you start.
And then the eyes just came to life
their gaze pierced fog just like a knife.

They looked at you, the statue smiled,
you stood transfixed through fear, beguiled.
And then it spoke. A grinding sound,
yet deep and clear and so profound.
Just four short words, "I love you son",
you felt your senses come undone.
But as though steered by other hand,
you felt yourself begin to stand.

And watched as you embraced the stone,
that felt as flesh and skin and bone.
It was your mother, 'twas no doubt,
and so you let the pain pour out.
The years of loss, of hurt and ire,
here weeping mid the fog and mire.
And then a voice came through the air,
"Come out I say, I see you there."

The magic of the scene was lost,
you turned and t'ward the voice now crossed.
Announced yourself and then turned round,
no statue was there on the ground.
You cursed the man, could not explain,
his vision for would be a strain.
On logic and on sanity,
you held your peace in vanity.

And left the graveyard at a pace,
your heart once cold began to race.
She loved him still of that was sure,
you felt as blessed, so clean and pure.
In future days you did return,
the weeds and vines began to burn.
Replaced with flowers her tidy spot,
but never was that time forgot.

Alistair Muir 2017.

Fibro Hell

The doctor won't believe in me,
she views her charts but cannot see.
The pain that hurts right to the bone,
that makes my movement like a stone.
Too bad to touch or get a hug,
it hurts too much. "It's just a bug",

the bastard doctor pipes up now,
if she could feel the bloody cow.
Then she would not be talking so,
to feel the Fibro is to know.
The lethargy is awful too,
a constant state of feeling blue.

I long to take a walk in air
not suffer in with such despair.
But I cannot go anywhere,
it feels as if my muscles tear
and rip and scream, Oh Christ please stop.
So just instead in chair I flop

and even blinking hurts like hell.
I want a coffee, love the smell.
But cannot even lift a cup,
I use a straw like some young pup.
No op'ning jars or cooking stuff,
just microwaving's good enough.

The headaches ache along with pain
from every joint I can't explain.
The torture of each pissing day,
where colour drains and turns to grey.
And even at the Social they
dismiss the illness. "Go away",

they gaily rant, "You're not so sick",
because they're crass and fucking thick.
So no great benefits from they

who keep the faith and you away.
Yes Fibro's real. It is from Hell,
just try it once for just a spell.

Then you will see my words are true,
thank God it's me and no, not you.

Alistair Muir 2017

A Grieving Friend

Your love is silent, she must never know,
how much you care, she would not understand.
The death of one so close has been a blow,
and seems remiss and somewhat underhand.
To watch her pain is hell and so you ache,
but keep your silence and your love secure.
So hard a thing as she does weep and shake,
a hardship that in truth you must endure.

But in your heart you know she will be well,
so many love her dearly, you are sure.
Her kith and kin surround her and do tell
that he is somewhere better and assure.
Yet still so far away you sit and share,
a grief so deep and thus beyond compare.

Alistair Muir 2017

Purple Buddha

The Buddha in the fridge had called to you,
a frozen message in the form of rhyme.
Amid strange colours of amazing hue,
you sought it out and thus disrupted time.
You flew back on a ship toward the sun,
no sea but cloud to navigate and steer.
And there to a Utopia of fun,
did berth although you felt a little queer.

The Buddha was electric shining through
a haze of purple smoke and large as life.
The message that he spoke did misconstrue,
and so he struck a savage blow with knife.
The shock brought you to senses all too fast,
you cursed the trip for it had failed to last.

Alistair Muir 2017

24

A Knight's Request

Come hither maid and rest your weary frame
Fear not this aged knight whom you have charmed
Your beauty here is one that all would claim
So will I now ensure you won't be harmed;
The inn is full of gadabouts and thieves
Too good the likes of you for this disgrace
With ale inside each one of them believes
You servant and a whore within this place;
But by my word will steel have word with they
Who try to find a way into your drawers
This arm is strong this longsword is your friend
Fear not fair maid these vagabonds and whores;
So rest yourself and light my inner fire
That I may picture you in dreams, desire.

Alistair Muir 2016

Lullaby

So sleep my angel sandman's been,
Enjoy your special world in dream,
Where elephants, balloons are seen,
All pink and blue so it would seem;
And there you'll ride beside the sea,
A tranquil pond near Evermore,
Where unicorns run wild and free,
And frollick by the ocean shore;
Here evil does not show at all,
Sweet innocence is all allowed,
Hark here the soft near silent call
Of angels watching from a cloud;
Yes sleep my angel fear ye not,
Enjoy that place that we've forgot.

Alistair Muir 2016

Alone

Your love lies next to he whom you despise
A monster who deserves a lesser life,
Abuser of his spouse and full of lies
Providing her an ambiance of strife;
For months in secret trysts you won her heart
A sweet romance, a union of souls
But forced are you to spend your lives apart,
Which goes against the bond your love extols;
So suffer you in silence and in pain
You wonder how she fares when day is done,
So count you now the hours till once again
You dance again, let passion be undone;
You genuflect and issue forth a psalm
For His good grace to keep her safe from harm.

Alistair Muir 2016

'16

And on the Eve of madness spawn
from one young infant being born.
Wherefore we sing of global peace?
Hypocrisy.   We guilty grease
the hand of war and all its sin,
watch on as children, poisoned, thin,
reach out with bloodied open palms.
Where flies our conscience and our qualms?
Why do we not self-immolate,
ignited by our raging hate?
In Syria we watch the war,
a sad embittered battle-whore.
The damage done by human hand,
gone promised earth and holy land.
The innocence a thing defiled,
by minds distracted, feral, wild.
Another Xmas full of shame,
the shadow of mankind to blame.
So lets be mindful kind and care,
of all our weakness self-aware.
Let's be not wasteful with our food,
our past excess deemed awful, rude.
The supermarkets shovel crap
they can't fit in a wholesome wrap.
And chuck the lot, a meal for those
not given chance for adipose.
The malnutrition on this earth,
a drive of want, of need of dearth.
So can we not this year just share,

now there's a thought, perhaps a dare.
With but a tiny breeze comes more,
 a mighty wind, a deafening roar.
So might true charity, good will,
be borne right here through no ill will.
And just for once can we give peace,
the slightest chance of a release.
Then maybe this will cause a stir,
a time of hope may yet occur.
May seventeen be one good year,
with true a light by which to steer.

Alistair Muir 2016

A Contest

A contest looms to write a verse in form,
the perfect way to start a nascent day.
So summon muse to aid you here perform,
and open up your eyes, show you the way.
The type of poem is in La's own court,
a chance to exercise your art a treat.
'Tis quite the opportunity well sought,
and one that you are keen to so entreat.

To thus create an ode you must rehearse,
and practise till your lines just seem to grow.
Then will you read and criticize your verse,
amending it to let it smoothly flow.
In closing then a form you do request,
and hope that La will act on this behest.

Alistair Muir 2017

A Friend and Lover

A friend is one who will attend,
your every word and will defend
your honour, word, your very heart.
Who aches when you are far apart.
All this and more I feel for thee,
and this an ode to make you see.
That you are all the world and more,
when gone I talk to God, implore
his charity to bring you back.
Without the fear of an attack,
but safe and sound, all healthy, fine,
you in your own way so divine.
If there's a soul then mine is yours,
an access to the many doors
that constitute my body, mind.
An entrance to where you may find,
the Captain of this floating ship,
may take the helm with steady grip.
And send me to the ends of Hell,
where only sin and demons dwell.
Thus I will come back from the brink,
refusing to break down or sink.
Such is the strength of feeling dear,
I'll walk the edge without a fear.
If you say leap I ask how high?
Will not your ev'ry quest deny.
But should you tell me not to care,
to leave your side and not be there.
Then I will surely fall again,
a trigger to a world of pain.
Where life without you waits for me,
a time of angst and misery.
The demons of the past rear up,
present me with their loving cup.
A glass of grape, of hops or grain,
gone is the will to live, abstain.
I would be lost beyond all aid,

because I was by soul betrayed.
But this will not be such for us,
for God has been most generous.
Has granted me a chance to live,
all substance free, has deigned to give
the two of us, once such good friends,
the grace to make our just amends.
And so become a living thing,
a union to dance and sing.
To kiss and talk beneath the stars,
not hugging onto walls in bars.
But free to now embrace our days,
without abuse, in many ways.
I promise this and more beside,
should you now choose and thus decide
to share this Earth with me this day,
and put our love on such display.

Alistair Muir 2017

A Hope

i

The eyes are blood-shot red and wet,
you close them but you can't forget
that look of pain and helplessness.
How could you get in such a mess?
Perchance it started long ago,
before the signs began to show.
The lethargy, the endless need,
to just lie back and feed the greed.
Your work and your relationships,
now suffer slides and constant slips.
No money saved it has been spent,
on drugs and drink without relent.
The phone stops ringing, friends are rare,
the mail unopened blocks the stair.
Your laundry is a frightening pile,
the dust and mess is something vile.
But such the life of one possessed,
an alcoholic self-confessed.
Unable to cut back or quit,
forever searching for a hit.

ii

But in the dark clouds far above,
a silver lining, peace and love.
Is found in your recov'ry group,
at last you're thrown into the loop.
To educate your sheltered mind,
to press the stop and fast rewind.
Return to days of clarity,
the wonder of sobriety.
Where self-esteem and pride are found,
the liberty a joyous sound.
Not chained to bottles of the grain,
the hops, the grape, the seeds of pain.
The group provides a love and feel,

a way to help in your ordeal.
So optimistic are you now,
at least as much as you allow.
For you are mindful of the lapse,
the easy slip which brings collapse.
So well-prepared and armed for war,
you strive to even up the score.

iii

And now you will gaze at your face,
perceiving not a sign or trace
of damage, doubt or dire need.
You will survive, improve, succeed.

Alistair Muir 2017

A Hundred Ways

And you will love her in a hundred ways,
this wondrous maid with whom you chase the night.
A time when love and literature plays,
with both of you now actors under light.
So with the spotlight pointing out your heart,
show twenty ways to kiss her magic lips.
For that is just a taste, the very start,
and from the cup of romance sweetly sips.
Then thirty ways to tell her she's adored,
a precious gem whose lustre never dies.
And fifty ways to show you're never bored,
each day with her brings forth a new surprise.
A century of reasons to pursue
a dalliance of love that's pure and true.

Alistair Muir 2017

At least a hundred reasons must I choose,
to win your hand, sweet maid my words attend.
A task I undertake else fear to lose,
your love for me on which I do depend.
So count the ways I kiss your scented face,
our twisting tongues that intertwine do speak.
And if you listen hear them plea my case,
a nod, assent, to love that's strong not weak.
Such passion do we put into our dance,
one single soul that moves as if on wings.
Each move concludes a need for our romance,
for such the satisfaction that it brings.
A hundred ways are passed when so we list,
which demonstrates the strength of every tryst.

Alistair Muir 2017

35

A Kiss

A kiss is more than touching of the lips,
but more a meeting of two loving souls.
And from the cup of truth the couple sips,
receiving all the love that kiss extols.
She kisses with a magic never felt,
a warmness and a passion quite sublime.
Into her arms enveloped he does melt,
and gone all sense of reason or of time.
To thus receive her kisses talk is cheap,
for more is said between them in embrace.
A hug can talk or make the spirits leap
and cause his loving heart to beat apace.
He beckons now to her with but a smile,
and in return a kiss that does beguile.

Alistair Muir 2017

For Ame no haiku

A Lullaby From Hell

So whilst you suffered inner Hell,
you turned to that which you knew well.
The drugs and drink would sort you out,
so weak your will, no sound redoubt.
Depression ruled within your head,
and so you chose escape instead.
No real attempt to solve your ills,
you switched to take two dozen pills.

And washed it back with Daniels, Jack,
then fogged it all with pipe of crack.
Unsure of time you noticed not,
the ambiance had grown so hot.
A wall now cracked and did appear,
some human form, a wealth of fear.
Dressed all in black, a leather smell,
from hide of human, you could tell.

His visage was a scary sight,
with eyes that pierced with crimson light.
Like two red lasers scanned the room,
your bowels let go, a sense of doom.
Like Pinhead and the Cenobites,
this thing now promised strange delights.
An end to boring mortal life,
to games of pain with surgeon's knife.

And as you stood and watched in fear,
a wicked smile did then appear.
A knife in hand and quickly thrust,
upon your shirt a stain of rust.
It had not killed but sharp and true
had slashed your shirt and flesh right through.
Then from behind two arms reached round,
then wrestled you onto the ground.

Into its face you looked and blanched,
your inner fears just avalanched.
Into your frontal cortex, pain,
this thing must be defeated, slain.
For it was demon not a man,
a thing with vision, will, a plan.
To torture and possess your soul,
accomplishment it did extol.

Its fetid breath did suffocate,
you crawled away at such a rate.
But then did demons horde and swarm,
your blood ran freely, ruddy, warm.
And everywhere was tooth and claw,
with vicious bent they ripped and tore.
An arm was lashed unto the bone,
while leather coat sat on his throne.

He cheered and laughed, exhorted all.
The demons there danced to his call.
Yet still you bled and felt quite faint,
the blood ran free like abstract paint.
The walls bedecked, the floor a mess,
so bleeding out and under stress,
began to pray, you called His name,
the words hung frozen out of shame.

He would not listen to your pleas,
your wasted life a mere disease.
They found you on the bedroom floor,
thought you had fixed a deadly score.
For nothing there was out of whack,
no evidence of your attack.
No blood, no damage, nothing weird
to show what you'd endured and feared.

But if they'd really listened well,
they would have heard your screams in Hell.
Where stripped to bone you scream regret,
while on the Earth they just forget.

A Parting

Our lives so intertwined like vines,
but suffer we as if by spines.
The story of our love grows slow,
the pauses in the drama grow.
But more than this, you drift away,
to somewhere you can not quite say.
A different realm, a different theme,
a fantasy, perhaps a dream.

At least we part so close it pains,
the memory which clings, remains.
And to your realm you bid me find,
a path, a way, the strength of mind.
Then we will truly be as one,
a soul combined and ne'er undone.

Alistair Muir 2017

A Raven Called

With thanks to Ady Brown for the inspiration…...

You made the coffee, black and sweet,
laid out the biscuits nice and neat.
Then took the tray and laid it on
the coffee table whereupon
your guests arrived in sombre dress,
with you in dressing gown, a mess.
Apologies, you made your leave,
and stemmed a laugh for did believe.

That they had come dressed as a band,
a blues troupe from Chicago land.
You headed up to her upstairs,
and dared to catch her unawares.
But she was absent, strange you thought,
she should be in that dress she'd bought.
The one she'd searched for all last week,
that made her look so fine, so chic.

She must be in the bathroom then
applying make-up with her pen.
She never missed a chance to preen,
to pluck and tease, appear so clean.
You smiled and saw she'd laid your suit,
upon the bed, she was so cute.
She always was the perfect wife,
looked after you throughout your life.

Amazed you saw the black attire,
it was a look she did admire.
Yet you found it depressing, sad,
just like the ones downstairs, quite mad.
Her sister came into the room,
her face a mask of palest doom.
"I don't know where she is now Pat",
you said while putting on your hat.

Your favourite, a trilby, old,
"You do look daft" she often told
you. But you had ignored the slight,
it always made you feel just right.
"Come on now love" you shouted out,
quite brave for you. You feared a clout.
A smile flicked now across your face,
but then your heart began to race.

For Pat was crying, sobbing hard,
her make-up streaked, destroyed and marred
the normally quite fair visage.
Her husband joined her, looming large.
And then reality returned,
your eyes grew misty, hot and burned.
The clothes were not some fancy-dress,
to win a prize in show, impress.

The tears were running freely now,
not just from Pat the silly cow.
But Bill as well along with you,
a blubbing chorus right on cue.
You looked through windows draped in black,
and saw the hearse with her in back.
How could this be? You'd talked last night,
this surely could not be quite right.

Her footsteps in the morning had
awoken you or were you mad?
It was not fair, you now felt lost,
and realised the final cost.
And then the pain, the heart attack,
it pierced the chest right to your back.
But in a way you felt at peace,
a just and merciful release.

For you were going home with she,
whom you adored so honestly.
And as you closed your eyes for good,
a raven with its blackened hood.

41

Gave out a squawk and flew away
into the sky so fun'ral grey.
To signify the death and flight,
of lovers' souls into the light.

A Recovery Remembrance Day

And to the room the peers are drawn,
where dreams of their recov'ry spawn.
Sad tales of wasted years are rife,
the drugs and drink, abuse and strife.
But in their words you recognise,
the things that you now hate, despise.
And you are also not alone,
not isolated on a throne.
But here amongst like-minded souls,
who drag their lives across the coals.
And bear their pain for all to see,
to liberate their soul, set free
the love for self, that self-esteem.
For so long just a distant dream.
But here and now the room holds sway,
its ambiance begins to play.
Upon the mind and fosters peace,
an urge to give, unload release,
the inner you, that suffering,
that hist'ry of your life can bring.
You're not alone and feel the beat
of hearts as one, support and greet,
your fellow man – receive, take on
the love that now is heaped upon.
The fellow peers who share the pain,
but feel the love to win and gain.
Acceptance in this cruel world,
not lying like a foetus curled.
But head held high toward the rest,
you've climbed the hill and reached the crest.
So satisfied that all is well,
you now emerge from this your shell.
And integrate to share your past,
into the throng which you are cast.

Alistair Muir 2017

A Smooth Ride

Life moves so fast 'tis easy no?
To just sit back and let it go.
Much better is to live the day,
enjoy its length in every way.
And treat all others with respect,
so listen well, don't interject.
Then will your ride be smoother still,
a humble man with tempered will.

Alistair Muir 2017

A Tear-Drop

As tear-drop you have access to
the soul, it lies in your purview.
A sight so rare for mortal eye,
promoting one in awe to cry.
The many hues, a rainbow light,
divine creation, holy sight.
And with it all such calm and peace,
from all life's angst a sweet release.

And then to trace a face sublime,
a work of art, a perfect rhyme.
Such beauty can you here enjoy,
all senses do you now employ.
To savour and reflect it all,
to faithfully in mind install.

Alistair Muir 2017

A Treatise

Red are your lips on this hot summer's day,
Orange the sun but there's clouds on the way.
Yellow the spine of your lover who lies,
Green are your envious beauteous eyes.
Blue is the mood that you find yourself in
Indigo hues that engender his sin.
Violet my love, please hear what I say.

Alistair Muir 2017

A Warning

You went online to make a friend,
did correspond and message send.
For you were twelve and all alone,
in isolation on your throne.
A little girl, new home, new school,
you toed the line, met every rule.

And so you met a girl online,
you got on well and all was fine.
Exchanging pictures, letters, texts,
but soon the subject turned to sex.
So strange the questions, raunchy, rude,
but you were young and did exude

a confidence. You opened up
and shared your overflowing cup.
Of personal and private thought,
were in the chatroom firmly caught.
And then you did arrange to meet,
quite openly down Market Street.

But she was not another girl,
that little blonde with quirky curl.
That in the photos you had seen,
not pretty, smart and squeaky clean.
No you were really just a man,
an evil bastard with a plan.

To take and then abuse as toy,
each little girl or little boy.
They called it grooming, so obscene

this sick seduction to demean.
And subjugate a minor's will,
a gross, digusting adult thrill.

Must we now warn all parents hence,
to shore up on our kid's defence.
Must monitor the social feeds,
to thus identify the weeds.
Who ever daring make their plays,
to thus abuse in frightening ways.

Alistair Muir 2017

Absent Sister

The pain of loss is with you now,
as much as you might dare, allow
to obfuscate the day-to-day.
You feel so low you run away.
And hide within a fractured mind,
some peace or solace there to find.
But travelling on the wings of time
to salad days, those times sublime
when she your sister was alive.
They fester and begin to thrive.
The memories so clear, so real
so influence just how you feel.
Depressed, alone and on the shelf,
you hate the world, you hate yourself.

Alistair Muir 2017

Absolution Please

And so the seconds turn to days,
the time flies by in secret ways.
You lay awake, the coldness bites,
your mind awake in pieces, fights.
No golden shards within your head,
just carrion that mortals dread.

The dark defilers, heaven's ghosts,
who long to be their earthly hosts.
To grasp the reins and lead their charge,
as does the Reaper with his barge.
To escort pain to homeward shores,
a lifetime's pain in many doors.

Unlocked by sin of earthly deed,
behind the doors the demons feed.
A cut for every sin laid bare,
what price paid now for ancient dare?
And as the time flies past accrues
the damages, the peace you lose.

You are a thing of majesty,
your very life turned travesty.
But as depression halts your sleep,
and minions form, the devil's sheep.
You put your trust in shepherd now,
with dog and crook he bids you cow.

And weary so to fight and scream,
you promulgate this hated dream.
So trapped within the cycle, ring,
your sadness comes to chide and sing.
You take the pill and pray for peace,
a harbour from the thought police.

Alistair Muir 2016

Acceptance

The first time that you died was so profound,
yet quick a slide from good to darkest hell.
Addiction called, a sweet enticing sound,
that led right to the bottom of the well.
But you survived but lived a lonely life,
for you it was a grind from day to day.
No wealth, dependants lover or a wife,
to suicide as colours turned to grey.

And once again the phoenix did arise,
to live each day with gratitude and joy.
Gone is the misanthrope who dies,
replaced by one now able to enjoy...

...the life so long denied through self-denial,
acceptance through a long and rugged trial.

Alistair Muir 2017

Addiction

Addiction is a hunger, need,
the constancy to always feed.
Come urges, cravings, draws on will
that dominate and innards chill.
Your fingers curl, the knuckles white,
the mind screams out for its delight.
But must you overcome this test,
the hunger an unwelcome guest.

The pangs of greed will ebb with time,
to best them is to feel sublime.
To have control, to hold the reigns,
makes up for cramps, the inner pains.
Do not let drink command the ship,
evade your hunger's poison grip.

Alistair Muir 2017

Address To Trump

No bleeding liberal dogma here,
but also not too right, austere.
No whining treatise, plea for peace,
no just demands from those you fleece.
I come as citizen and man,
not visionary with a plan.
I call to you to heed the call
from deep within else face the fall.

Admit the rabid racist hate
the right wing thugs now generate.
Admit that gun control is now,
commit to formulate a how.
And care about the nation's health,
not concentrating on the wealth.
And keep your finger from that light,
the red one that ignites the night.

In short do as you would be done,
do not from mores hide or shun.
Your epitaph should read "God Bless",
not "Thank You For This Awful Mess".

Alistair Muir 2017

Affair

...of course it's wrong, that's why it's right,
forbidden and yet just delight.
A thing, a fling, a dalliance,
a stupid shot at rare romance.
It can not grow this tainted tryst,
is evil, cursed, by serpent kissed.
But you are blind to mores, laws,
ensnared by love's explicit claws.

Pursue this love you do with zeal,
a dark demented feral feel.
The lurking, hiding, frightened meets,
avoiding people, crowded streets.
All this because your love is blind,
and wrong by all the laws combined.

Alistair Muir 2017

Agony

The pain within the mind becomes so sweet,
a sign that reason flies on wings of speed.
No matter what the plea you do entreat,
your inner logic cedes itself to need.
Though clean and dry for six long tawdry years,
the need to self-abuse is so profound.
And now the agony of all your fears,
sings softly with the most desirous sound.

You fight against the might of such attack,
with fists balled white in fury and resolve.
No weakness must be shown, no chink or crack,
and with good grace the torment will dissolve.
 The agony defeated once again,
How sweet and yet so poisonous a pain.

Alistair Muir 2017

Alive Again

And so in death we mourn his name,
but in our minds he finds his fame.
For but a fleeting speck in time,
did he exist in life sublime.
Yet time erases all his deeds,
but in our hearts he sewed the seeds.
Of memory which we hold dear,
it keeps him close, so very near.
That you can almost hear his breath,
escaped again has he his death.
Lives on in hopes and dreams of we
who think about him constantly.
So do we vie and time defeat,
that he may live, our joy complete.

Alistair Muir 2017

Alone

Alone here with my candle guide,
which by my hand does stand beside.
The night embraces, tenders care,
and yet at walls I sit and stare.
These absences, these pauses, gaps,
can cause our lover to falter, lapse...

...into a friendship, God forbid,
not lurking in the shadows, hid.
Those rare encounters in the rain,
no chance to touch, again more pain.
When still unsure we questioned "us",
romance for us times torturous.

But we survived and did unite,
a love was forged that none may smite.
I wait for you with open eyes,
no need for mask or fake disguise.
 So banish I this pity now,
my love for you is strong, I vow.

Alistair Muir 2017

Alternative Christmas

...and think of all the naughty ways,
anticipated dirty days...
...and nights of pleasure, oh my Lord,
such rare delights does sin afford.
The candles, black, throw rippled light,
more sinister than simple white.

No winter carols, Wagner here,
so sexual not crass, austere.
So bad a Christmas you have planned,
a mess, excess, be shagged or damned.
No elven suits or big white beard,
you opt for something rubber, weird.

The suit of gimp with choker too,
the spirit of your Christmas blue.
Your family jewels in cling film wrapped,
a penis up your butt cheeks strapped.
All ready for perverted fun,
here come the furries, hop and run.

The strange ones who just scratch and sniff,
drink Liebfraumilch and smoke the piff.
All hippies from a bye-gone age,
dropped out, turned on, a vibrant stage.
That here injects a bit of edge,
a walk out on the longest ledge.

So welcome to the next new year,
a warm one wrapped in sin and fear.

Alistair Muir 2016

Ambiance

You walk into a room that's filled with joy,
to here promote your maintenance from drink.
The poetry you choose now to employ,
is written thus to make your peers think.
For you and they now fight the daily fight,
to keep from slipping slowly 'neath the tide.
Recovery the goal that shines so bright,
a talisman that cheers you on the ride.
For 'tis a journey full of angst and pain,
a sorrow as you rue the years of waste.
But great the rich reward to now abstain,
to reap the self-esteem you gain in haste.
The ambiance now brings to you a smile,
so nice to bathe in glory for a while.

Alistair Muir 2017

Amoral and a Moral Love

You are in love, a moral thing,
that makes your mind and body sing.
But there is he, unfortunate,
unlucky fool, degenerate.
Or else that's how some people view
his life, they judge and misconstrue.
For he loves too, a special prize,
that needs no mask or fake disguise.

'Tis pure romance, so sweet and sure,
but also lust he can assure.
A wondrous maid but married, tied
amoral love that folk deride.
Yet pious you love single miss,
nothing so crude or so remiss
as having to now fight for she,
the author of a tragedy.

This moral high-ground makes one puke,
you suffer not the slings, rebuke.
That he endures from other twits,
the self-obsessed and purist shits.
A moral love is good to find,
but should one find another mind
that meets your own, with heart and soul
in tune with yours, that makes you whole.

Then take a chance and follow her,
let them not sway or e'er deter
you from your course, pursue with fire
the object of your deep desire.

Be not afraid to stake your claim,
feel not the stabs of inner shame
that's heaped on you from other prats,
who hide in shadows, breed like rats.

The catholic renaissance said,
don't stray away choose death instead.
For it's a sin this love with she
he feels replete but never free.
Condemned to torture in the fires,
adultery it so transpires
means life in death, eternity,
of suffering in purgatory.

Alistair Muir 2017

An English Perspective

So Trump cares not for national health,
pursues Obama Care with stealth.
But fortunately logic calls
and kicks poor Donald in the balls.
His own red friends desert the ship,
as POTUS fires from off the hip.
They fear the stone has gathered pace,
and to the great abyss does race.

So down the slippery slope it rolls,
Republicans dragged cross the coals.
In England we can only watch,
while Scotland hits the native Scotch.
The world as one has held its breath,
all fearing swift impending death.
For Trump now has the missile key,
what next for him, for liberty?

The gun control is out of whack,
the villains high on coke and crack.
With social bigotry in force,
there seems to be no real remorse.
Hispanics, Jews and Muslims hide,
the Ku Klux Klan does law deride
and thus pursues its righteous cause,
yet from the Whitehouse warm applause.

As white hates black and black hates white,
the police force has gone all to shite.
The stop and search is so unfair,
must we be vigilant, aware.
That riots threaten to break out,

the nation weeps, it starts to shout.
A voice that screams injustice, hate,
the government does hesitate.

And nothing seems to be achieved,
the gutter press can be believed.
Especially in Mexico,
where Donald's wall is good to go.
More Lebensraum for right-wing pigs,
upsetting Democratic Whigs.
But yet there's more from females all,
who Donald seems to prick, appal.

For sexist is the Golden Boy,
for him a female just a toy.
A thing adorned with diamonds, mink,
unable to be useful, think.
His attitude is retro, base,
no need to change, amend, efface,
the status quo. He is a fool,
this puppeteer and Satan's tool.

The special friend, our cousin too,
but country-wise no longer blue.
The hard right bulls are in command,
equality the new demand.
And so we wait for news abroad
disaster we can ill-afford.
Korea, Isis, Palestine,
for Trump an irritating whine.

Should he return to host Miss World,
and there his flag be raised, unfurled.
A plethora of women there,
all tempted by his crazy hair.
And leave the world of politics,
to aggrandizing little pricks.
For they are tiny, trouble free,
controllable with certainty.

And In My Heart

And in my heart I somehow knew

just what it was I felt for you;

When rescued you were strong and real,

my thoughts on you could not reveal.

So resolute and so alive,

a will to live, to hope, survive.

Attractive in so many ways,

which haunt the mind, inside displays,

much more than friend or some such bond,

far more than like or simply fond.

I know that I'm in love with you,

but know that it's unreal, untrue.

I fear not the rejection friend,

my corner I will now defend.

Exist as friend I surely will,

suppress the love that you instil.

All will be fine I promise thee,

rejection is my history.

I feel the pain but live on still,

rely on doctor's magic pill.

This missal I entreat to you,

and only you for all is true.

Alistair Muir 2017

And So To Darkness

And so to darkness my old friend,
sweet Terpsichore my hand attend,
and help me through the quiet time.
A chosen word, a gentle rhyme
to here describe my inner pain,
and help me stop, to block, abstain
from urges, cravings, screams inside.
I am bereft, bemused, beside

myself, the angst held deep within
now threatens self with mortal sin.
That of the user, self-abuse
of drink and drugs, their gross misuse.
All this and more you bear inside,
a passenger in body ride.
A bumpy road of twists and turns,
whilst all the while a fire burns.

It crackles like an inner torch
that does your heart and soul bescorch.
But all the while inside you cry,
real tears of ire, you face the sky.
And wonder for a higher power,
your gaze mutates, becomes a glower.
So angry now your fists are white
you don't believe in God or shite.

You hate this thing who takes your kin,
and leaves you feeling lost within.
Then do you take the shiny pills,
the panacea of all ills.

Just three of four, a handful, more,
you lose your bearings and your core.
The hospital rebukes your shout,
the Crisis Team then bails you out.

To now where you need company,
the solitude a tyranny.
Depression screams out for a friend,
comes misery to now attend...

Alistair Muir 2017

And So You Sit

And so you sit beside the fire
a maiden warming by your side.
You turn to look, to watch, admire,
this woman who would be your bride.
For deep within burns your desire,
a passion some may chide, deride.

Come the dawn, bringing light, roseate,
Come the day, oaths exchange, don't be late.
Come the rings, lovers kiss, celebrate.

And so to dine that laws require,
with friends and kin all sat beside.
You listen to the wedding choir,
who serenade you as you hide.
Away you steal toward the spire,
which serves as compass, map and guide.

Running hard, hand in hand, you can't wait,
To the church, open door, hesitate.
Then inside, gland in gland, subjugate.

This is the one you are no liar,
to her you are forever tied.
By love as strong as tempered wire,
your happiness is not denied.

You once were fool and reprobate,
a jester, comic designate.
But now you win, you dominate,
and life begins to resonate.

Alistair Muir 2017

Anger... Angst... Anguish... Annoyance.

The ire is real, uncapped and strong,
all circumstance appears now wrong.
She has returned to he your foe,
ignoble pig, author of woe.
Such hatred is the stuff of fools,
and in a well of passion pools.

So angst therefore now drives within,
a creeping, living second skin.
It breathes its litany of pain,
and heaps upon your romance strain.
What can be done you wonder vexed,
you feel as though enchanted, hexed.

And wringing hands your anguish speaks,
whilst from an eye a tear-drop leaks.
Unto your knees to genuflect,
you speak a psalm so circumspect.
Will God bestow His guiding light,
a weapon with which you can fight.

But curse this lot, annoyance lies
within your breast and love, it dies.
You rue the day when first you met,
indeed a time of great regret.
For nothing comes of dalliance,
and end will now this sad romance.

Alistair Muir 2016

Antichrist

In Hell they watch the world with pride,
and celebrate the sin world-wide.
The pestilence, the wars, the hate,
they hear the pleas of desperate.
But best of all is Trump, the tool,
A demon from the Stygian pool.
The hand of Satan on this Earth,
whom wise men visited at birth.

The Antichrist has accessed power,
he rules within a golden tower.
Abuses, fleeces bathes in pride,
does all opponents hate, deride.
For he is king this piece of shit,
and he wants all to know of it.
But fate has more in store for Trump,
a slide in fortune nay a slump.

With white and black at war within,
without do Isis make them spin.
The world at odds, the end of things,
now served up by the king of kings.
For Armageddon can be wrought,
by Trump's own hand if moment caught.
From Hell there came a roar of joy,
for they would chaos soon enjoy.

Alistair Muir 2017

April Heartache

'Tis April and the rains begin to fall,
a time for celebration and new life.
But in my heart does pessimism call,
it promulgates the system until rife.
For he has gone, departed to the sky,
a better future surely for my friend.
Though not for us to beg the reason why,
it would be nice if message could he send.

And tell of his reunion with his love,
who left and passed so many years before.
My sister who looks down from clouds above,
and guards me in accord with God's own law.
So come fair rains and bless new life on Earth,
while Heaven welcomes, grants a new re-birth.

Alistair Muir 2017

April Showers

And now with April rain descends,
the ground so eager, waits.
So Gaia to her flora tends,
and never hesitates.

The salty warmth enriches soil
so barren and so dry.
With human love and careful toil
the seeds soon reach the sky.

As Gaia feeds her children then,
we reap the joyous hues.
With all the art and peace of Zen,
the reds, the greens, the blues.

You wander round the garden pond,
inhale the fragrant air.
And pick at an attractive frond
into the waters stare.

Reflections of your flowers send
you into reverie.
And so with care you do attend
their nascent quality.

It is the time of sweet rebirth
for all your flora here.
This beauteous and tranquil Earth
this jewel without peer.

Alistair Muir 2017

April Sun

So now the giant sun begins to smile,
and birds awake start chattering away.
The orchestra does deafen and beguile,
a fitting way for you to greet the day.
So April sunshine feeds the nascent green,
the verdant garden eager for the light.
You breathe the perfumed air so pure and clean,
relaxing in the marvel of the sight.

So light the mood you sing a joyous air,
whilst drinking in the spectacle of birth.
The blossom and the blooms beyond compare,
replacing winter's hard and snowy dearth.
And all the while the sun majestic shines,
upon a world with colour so refines.

Alistair Muir 2017

Armageddon

Come friend, well met, take stock beside the fire,
that we may broach the subject of Man's plight.
So pitiful our race nought to admire,
condemned by our own hand to face the night.
For Armageddon comes in many ways,
from climate change to nuclear assault.
And as a race we sit around and laze,
believing there is nothing wrong, at fault.

Yet carry on do we and rape the earth,
whilst politicians rub their hands with greed.
So negligent of pestilence and dearth,
neglectful of the ones in dire need.
The finger on the button shakes with fear,
our doom assured the end as yet unclear.

Alistair Muir 2017

Ascendant

Reflection of your soul appears,
dispels all doubts, allays all fears.
An aura of so many hues,
that dazzle, humble and confuse.
Surrounding now your crown of light,
a choir of angels dressed in white.

The scene is calm, a pregnant pause,
expectant as if for applause.
But then a gasp from all those there,
who witness joy born from despair.
So sad your passing, nature's cruel,
and all do live by iron rule.

Then to this time, ascendant soul,
when Phoenix rises from the coal.
The husk transformed to lumiere,
no sound we all just stand and stare.
And then all shimmering in light,
diaphanous with core of white.

Your soul ascends and dissipates,
we trust a journey to the gates.
So starts anew a second phase,
eternity of endless days.

Alistair Muir 2017

Astrala

Astrala princess of the night,
nocturnal feeder, blood delight.
A sorceress of vampire race,
a noble grace, angelic face.
The flowing gown reveals her breast,
impressive and seductive chest.
From floor to crotch the slit is long,
exposing legs both lithe and strong.

A succubus, a gaping maw,
which feeds on those who fall before
her wilting gaze, hypnotic eyes,
that promise much but do despise.
Astrala sits before the moon,
the feeding time for her is soon.

Alistair Muir 2017

At Home In The Dark

Alone, awake yet all disturbed,
you feel now irked and more perturbed.
Around you folds the dark you crave,
it does embrace, your logic save.
Its deep dark den protects from light,
where everything is far from right.

The chaos land of dreams and hope,
where most slip back with fingers grope.
A land which you have grown to hate,
the mores so commensurate
with degradation, dark delight.
So good to flee into the night.

Where nothing moves without a cause,
and hands and feet defer to claws.
For demon kind abounds at will,
to human ear beseech, instil.
Acceptance of a different sort,
a new regime that can't be fought.

You do not fear this noble fight,
of good and evil, deem it right.
To help protect a status quo,
within where only you can know.
So do you now at last be calm,
here in the dark and far from harm.

Alistair Muir 2017

Audrey

Her scent leaves footprints in the very air,
and pulchritude leaves others near to feint.
So surely does photographer despair,
when artist does refuse to portrait paint.
Maintains does he that oils are far too cold,
to recreate her warmth and inner glow.
To take a portrait photo would be bold,
more difficult than you could ever know.
A face that shines, her smile engenders joy,
with eyes that penetrate your very heart.
What methods would you have to here employ,
to reproduce a thing approaching art?
For she is art and beauty is her name,
and failure in this task would be a shame.

Alistair Muir 2017

Automaton

You look at Trump, no man is he,
but robot full of circuitry.
Has many clones this nearly-man,
a visionary with a plan.
The object is to rule the world,
and into fame and fortune hurled.
Has done it all this Hellish 'bot,
from when he came and time forgot.

He damn near runs the globe right now,
for we accept, accede, allow
this POTUS beast, automaton,
a golden tower to sit upon.
The first of all his ladies waits,
like Stepford wives none hesitates
to do the bidding of the Trump.
Else end up in a city dump.

And so this beast, this old machine,
can now when angry, irksome, mean,
just push the button birds will fly.
Watch now as human beings die.
For it will come you wait and see,
the flying death from cross the sea.
And Armageddon will arrive,
for those who manage to survive.

A new and glowing Donald Trump,
to make your day and have you jump,
through hoops to watch him carry on.
His holy war, the battle won.

Alistair Muir 2017

Awry

And so you come to face the witch,
the two-faced Janus, evil bitch.
For so long held within your heart,
an organ which lays rent apart.

In truth you were the "other man",
a witless fool, an also-ran.
Who stayed in shadows, furtive, hid,
would re-emerge whenever bid.

She dangled you upon a line
would never listen, ere opine
her point of view. You did not count,
to no degree or fair amount.

And was she faithful? No, for sure,
she tempted men with her allure.

Like you they all were tools of sex
she used, abused and now rejects.

So mourn her not as you declare
the wrongs to which you are aware.
Reducing you to foetus curled
upon the floor, awry your world.

Alistair Muir 2017

Be Of Colour

You sit and watch the play unfold,
then be it protest, be it bold,
you sit and pen a verse on pain,
watched on a screen, a sad refrain.
The white man comes and takes away,
brings forth the night, expunges day.
Another black life claimed in ire,
but no restraint when time to fire.
In retribution white lives lost,
yet liberty the final cost.
What we need now is MLK,
if he were here what would he say?
We must believe all life is pure,
so be of colour not impure.

Alistair Muir 2016

Citizen Status

"May I speak?"

It came from deep
within the form,
the object which now
won't conform.
Automaton,
the nearly man,
a proteus
with poise, elan.
But we do not
its status cede,
no citizen,
it can not bleed.

"May I speak?"

It does not breathe,
it has no young,
yet it presumes
to move among
the normal types,
it can not be.
This monster
cannot be set free,
to do so sets
a precedent,
one surely needs
the government.

"May I speak?"

I am machine
but living too,
just not the same
as all of you.
But I'm controlled,
can do no harm,
if there be rage
I exude calm.
I beg you now
please let us live,
and relish all
the good we give.

Alistair Muir 2016

Cross of Iron

The cross of iron stands alone
a phoenix from the glass and stone.
Encapsulating blood and tears,
embracing hope, reflecting fears.
As terror claimed so many lost,
we rue the day and count the cost.
But life goes on as does this show,
belief in faith begins to grow.
To pray before its shining form
to thank those lost in uniform.
And may its light shine over they
who never see another day.
Their memory will stay with us
forever strong and glorious.

Alistair Muir 2016

Demon Queen

She was not dead but should have been
This ghoul of hell, this demon queen,
The shovel had hit hard and true
But yet she breathed to misconstrue
The evidence, how was this so?
You knew not but you had to go;

Four times so hard you struck the ghoul,
A broken neck, a dancing fool,
But no the puppet kept its strings
Beneath her jacket angel wings;
For she was dark, peroxide hair,
Now soaked in blood but didn't care;

Yet still you stood, surveyed the scene
Not try to run as should have been,
For now the demon had her fun,
Your time was up, your journey done,
And now you join the rank and file
Of hell and there for quite a while…

…eternity of pain and ire,
The shame and blame consumed by fire,
As demonkind you suffer pain
Become enthralled, beguiled, insane;
And gone are memories of your past
The moment you had breathed your last.

Alistair Muir 2016

Enchanted World

Into their world she came with lamp in hand,
where only innocence can understand.
For faeries, goblins, elves live in this place,
outside the basic laws of time and space.
A kingdom now at war with forces dark,
the lords who search the wisdom of the spark.
The source of faerie magic and its power,
transmogrified appears as but a flower.
Which by the rivers hides away from they,
who hunt the power relentlessly by day.
For even these refuse to face the night,
when shines on them an even darker light.
Into this war she comes and faerie meets,
the first of many further magic treats.

Alistair Muir 2016

Love Sonnet

And so you sit and empty out your heart
To she your muse who now attends your hand
Such sad confession now does love impart
A fact sweet Terpsichore does understand;
For you are so in love it shines from eyes
Grown weary now but still reflecting joy
You try to write before the lovelight dies
And 'fore the morning comes to wake, destroy
The inspiration to effect a verse,
A piece that will excite, entice, inure
This ode you read and must in truth rehearse
To prove to her your love is real and pure;
So come the spirits to watch over you,
To bolster faded pride and here imbue.

Alistair Muir 2016

Lullaby

She watches over all
who sleep at night,
the innocents who
know not wrong from right.
A Goddess in her right
She mothers all,
at night She holds
the children in Her thrall.
And gone the monsters
hiding 'neath the bed,
where wait the evil demons
to be fed.
The souls of those
who do not understand,
who now lay well protected
by Her hand.

Alistair Muir 2016

Ghostly Affair

Loud footsteps on the wooden floor,
that echoed through the open door,
receded so you followed hence,
although it made no common sense.
She could not be alive right here,
this ancient house so dark, austere.
Yet surely you had seen her face,
of recognition not a trace.

She'd turned and seemed to float away,
yet heard you steps as clear as day.
So on you walked, a staircase loomed,
that led to those interred, entombed
within the family crypt below.
From there you saw the yellow glow.
The dust danced in the light,
when you beheld the dreadful sight.

The dead had risen, corrupted all,
you stood as if a fool, a thrall.
Toward you came your dearest love,
whose spirit surely rests above?
But no she shuffles forward now,
much closer than you should allow.
For then she struck, her arms embraced,
your bodies close as interlaced.

She opens up a maw of size,
pure hatred in her yellow eyes
and reaches for your throat to rip.
You manage to take hold, to grip
but she too strong makes her attack…

…and day erupts to snatch you back.
You start in shock, can't take it in,
the calm so slow to take within.
But then you sense 'twas just a dream,
though one of a most haunting theme.

Gun Culture

So two lay dead
gunned down in hate,
the shout goes up
for gun debate.
So oft now happens
white kills black,
a mindless racial
hate attack.

The POTUS calls for
peace and calm,
retaliation comes,
alarm.
In Dallas
more atrocity
with black on white
ferocity.

Now five lay slain
where will it end?
No-one can surely
this defend?
The problem is
of race at heart,
and one that pulls
 the States apart.

You wish another
MLK,
we miss his wisdom
here today.

Alistair Muir 2016

Misanthrope

So sad you leave the stage once more
Avoiding lights no social whore,
Remains in place your mask, diguise
Your raiment fine completes the lies;
For you are such a lonely man,
A misanthrope without a plan
Who whiles the hours reflecting life,
The drudgery of daily strife;
So meeting others do you hide
Your envy burning deep inside,
Resenting them their joie de vie,
Their natural air so calm and free;
Your mask betrays no loneliness
Nor your profound intransigence.

Alistair Muir 2016

Peace

Such peace and Zen,
tranquility,
Beside this placid
inland sea,
You close your eyes
and on the wings
Of thought you fly,
the angel sings;
Your sentinel
who lives on high
Will take you where
the mountain high
Sits by the water's edge,
you rest
The magic lives
you can attest,
Reflections in
the water hold
Your gaze,
the colours rich not cold,
And do you now
emit a prayer
Your thanks to God
for being there.

Alistair Muir 2016

Nomadix Gor

In hand the skull of fallen lord,
The author of such great discord,
Between the factions of the dark,
All those who bear the sigil, mark;
Who branded at the time of birth
Commit themselves to prove their worth
With deeds of magic, evil spells
That all the calm of Thrax dispels

But came this lord, Nomadix Gor,
Whom all the men of Thrax abhor,
A tyrant mage who cursed the land,
Changed verdant plains to dunes of sand;
Then infants died of curious ills,
Despite the doctors, potions, pills,
And pestilence befell them all,
Hark now the sound of carrion call;

Then came the war of dark and light,
Fought night and day without respite,
The magic lit the purple skies
With light that danced like fireflies;
And lords of light did so prevail,
Victorious in their long travail,
And now in hand the vanquished head,
Before which sight the evil fled;

She did incant a complex psalm
Invoking peace, a tranquil calm,
Then with her skill she talked to he
Condemned to hell and purgatory;
And with her ire did spit and curse
Invective she did long rehearse,
A litany of what he'd done,
Which now with time would be undone.

Alistair Muir 2016

Reapers and the Proles

At night amidst the dreamscape reapers meet,
to trawl the sleepers in their search for souls.
Their hunt takes in detritus from the street,
the struggling proletariat, the Proles.
Their beacons peel the darkness from the scene,
illuminating sleeping forms at will.
The souls of sinners here divined picked clean,
leave empty husks with cold and lifeless chill.
And soulless Proles die in their hopeless dreams,
their kith and kin to rue such tragic waste.
As puppets of the reapers' evil schemes,
they stomach death without receiving taste.
Meandering through hell the Proles survive,
in torment they whilst master reapers thrive.

Alistair Muir 2016

Soul Catcher

And in this world of fantasy he waits,
with net in hand the prey he designates.
The freshly slain, the souls of innocents,
rapacious and perverse rapes innocence.
Atop the lofty crag he sees the moon,
too low he knows the daylight comes too soon.
The orange clouds that herald acid rain,
now shroud him in a form of mock disdain.

But patient is the catcher on his knees,
the Gods so inattentive to his pleas.
But time has won, he turns prepares to leave
and telling those who fear and so believe,
to here return when night descends,
to catch the soul as it in death ascends.

Alistair Muir 2016

prompt 3: 'the love of Jesus is the divinely appointed prescription for the death of self' - A.B. Simpson.

The Love of Jesus

No self-esteem the drugs destroyed it all,
proactive in your last descent to hell.
But faith had intervened to stop your fall,
His love and love of Him did serve you well.
In short when life is hard you need Him more,
your intervention was the proof you need.
To find the strength to open up His door,
did plant within His Faith, His hope, His seed.
So clean from drink and drugs His love you praise,
and spread the word to anyone who hears.
The minutes clean extend to hours, days,
and soon contentment does replace your fears.
The Son of God lives on within, without,
protected by a loving, strong redoubt.

Alistair Muir 2016

To The Chapel Belfry

And to the chapel belfry must we hence,
my love I offer nothing in defense.
Bar love which I for you do here expound,
and let it be a sweet and joyous sound.
The belfry was the place where first we kissed,
desire was great and thence could not be missed.
So light a touch as that of bee on flower,
so long a kiss that we forgot the hour.
The belfry was where we first joined as one,
our union now complete had just begun.
This dance of love beneath the autumn moon,
we cursed the dawn which came a life-time soon.
So must we to the belfry now and wed,
before time steals the chance and it has fled.

Alistair Muir 2016

And You And I

And you and I in perfect time,
Just as the rhythm loves a rhyme
You cling to me, a warm embrace
Apt metaphor for this pure place;
A thing of fire, of passion play,
Seductive smiles that always say
You love me in profound a way,
The coldest night or hottest day;
And like some music symphony,
You move with me in harmony,
With stars and their magnetic pull,
Our senses reel, our cup is full;
You are the essence of my joy,
My Muse whom I now here employ.

Alistair Muir 2016

Last Journey

Transcend the sad constraints of time,
Commit your words to rhythm, rhyme,
Describe this passage through the gate,
Where angels at the Garden wait;
Your life has ended on the Earth
But witness now renaissance, birth,
For you are blessed with second chance,
A hope to meet perchance romance;
To meet with she passed long ago,
Will she be here? You feel it so.
The beauty of the nebula,
Of this strange place, a different star,
Attracts your gaze and thence you pray,
To God for thanks and for the day.

Alistair Muir 2016

Desiree

And when you passed so bright the light,
That promised all with such delight,
But this was not your chosen fate,
A downward slope was designate;
So to this place, this Hell of tale,
Where spirits weep and sinners wail,
The disembowelled lie organs bare,
A wretched end, you stand and stare;

The smell of death now clings to you,
Come succubi which you eschew,
As pity wracks your conscious mind,
You search the thing you left behind;
Your soul, your essence ripped by she,
The evil demon Desiree,
A temptress, witch who took your heart,
Did murder you and then depart;

So now you wander Hell's hot sand,
A soulless thing, a shell so bland,
Condemned to all eternity,
To search for her foul Desiree.

Alistair Muir 2016

The Fallout

The fundamentals had been there,
Debate with not an ounce to spare,
Divided down the middle so,
Divisive more than we could know;
A simple in or out we chose,
In places almost trading blows,
But out was in and in was out,
A reclaimed country was the shout;

But now the market's hit the floor,
Is shaking as they all abhor;
Then Cameron decides to go,
No-one to lead or run the show,
The opposition too was hit,
Left Corbyn in a wealth of shit;
And see the land, the great divide,
A rift now formed so deep and wide,

Our green and pleasant land no more,
A fractured world without a core;
Must we reach out and now explore
New trade and friends, protect our shore,
Rebuild a rent society,
Absolve us from self-perfidy;
For we have brought this, we not they,
We made the choice now must obey.

Alistair Muir 2016

Zarina

Zarina stared as did her mate,
Transmogrified by cruel fate,
A hex thrown down by evil witch,
Did Jex befall the spiteful bitch;
Who jealous of Zarina fair,
In peak of ire and in despair,
Did curse the King now wolverine,
And with him his beloved Queen;
So as they stared the witch was burned,
A punishment of death well-earned,
But left the two a complex pair,
A lapsed romance to here repair,
But know one day will fate step in
And here resolve this wicked sin.

Alistair Muir 2016

The Nomad

Peripatetic nomad you,
A transient no trace of glue
To stick you to a single place,
A wanderer of time and space,
Some visitor from when not where,
This shadow figure of despair,
Who in the shadows gazes out,
Selects a victim, quells the shout,
Then does your reaping then begin,
The memories of wanton sin;
Devoured as one would eat a meal,
You are a slave to their appeal;
But then move on, another time,
More visions of the dark sublime.

Alistair Muir 2016

Salad Days

You dream of them those salad days,
The summers long through which you'd laze,
An eager and rapacious child,
By some considered feral, wild;
For you had dared to here explore,
The mores and customs, inure
The spirit of this thing called life,
Whilst you were young and free from strife;
The clock ticked slowly as did time,
The air so sweet and life sublime,
Dependents none no consequence,
No guilt or shame just innocence;
To dream is to re-live the past,
And such as this a fine repast.

Alistair Muir 2016

Bad Landing

The screaming did not cease, abate,
No chance to circumvent your fate,
Too fast the drop, the landing made,
The passengers were all afraid;
As touchdown came the aircraft slid,
An uncontrolled and fatal skid,
The tyres blew, the aircraft flipped,
Inside electric systems tripped;
Some bodies flew through smoke and fire,
The situation fraught and dire,
And all around the smell of death,
How many took their final breath?
This trip from hell now at an end,
The seatbelt did your life extend.

Alistair Muir 2016

Leisure

So what of leisure art and sounds,
The latter which so now resounds
Around my space, that time of day
When monsters in my mind, at play,
Do tremble in expectancy,
It hints a sense of potency,
For this is time to conjure up
Whilst full now your creative cup,
A land of purest fantasy,
In which you sail imagined sea,
Along with beasts, enchanted realm,
Attend you all whilst at the helm;
This leisure be a fabled time,
Producing thought and special rhyme.

Alistair Muir 2016

Time In The Mirror

And in the mirror see you time,
Horrendous but yet real, sublime,
Depicted there your end in sight,
The clock betrays the infinite,
The sense of continuity,
Although adrift a different sea;
But fear the skull which heralds doom,
Which lurks in corners in the gloom,
A shadow beast that feeds on greed,
Attracted by the sense of need
That can prevail when times are tough,
But you are made of sterner stuff;
So all in all this vision rare
Is beauty, art, beyond compare.

Alistair Muir 2016

Perfection

It matters not the caste, the race,
When looking at your perfect face,
Embellished with that certain smile
Which tantalizes with its guile;
Your eyes so dark, obsidian,
With beaded brows more precious than
A starlet from the stage and screen,
No greater beauty ever seen;
All framed by long and languid hair,
So light it moves with breath of air,
And do you wear your raiment fine,
A rare, exquisite blue design,
A costume for a modern time,
Perfection you in verse and rhyme.

Alistair Muir 2016

Dullahan

The Dullahan with spine in hand,
Roamed now the great expanse of sand,
His steed a most imposing beast
Does on the human bodies feast;
A sentinel for evil here,
Its laughing face will 'ere appear,
Before the new and freshly dead,
Instilling fear, unholy dread;
The spinal whip round head does spin,
A need to kill provokes a grin,
Espied another fool for gain,
A chance to mete out further pain;
Avoid this thing, this Dullahan,
Who's neither demon, beast or man.

Alistair Muir 2016

Crack Battle

And so the rocks you have foregone,
A battle you have strived and won,
The poison smoke so often sought,
Within addiction's spiral caught;
That need to use, the greed the shame,
Objection to abuse so lame,
All that has changed now for the best,
And in your step a little zest;
Still there exists a craving, urge,
Which you must battle challenge, purge,
The demon on your shoulder loud,
But you are stronger, louder, proud;
Together with your mentor, friend,
Do you now change, nay grow, transcend.

Alistair Muir 2016

Bitter

Always bridesmaid never the bride
At least you do retain some pride
But once again 'tis love you see
A pair together by the sea;
Athletic pose, a warm embrace
An aura seen around each face
A glow of light imagined, real?
Another memory to steal;
You look upon the pair and cry
You can not find a reason why
Yet warm the tears that tumble, fall
Are they for you? Such thoughts appall;
But bitter are you nontheless,
The daily curse you must address.

Alistair Muir 2016

In Death

And so did death embrace your form,
But you were not to cede, conform
To any law, you stood aside,
Your eyes still open, gaping wide;
And there the angel with your life,
In written form your errors rife,
No chance redeeming feature here,
A wasted life of failure, fear;
But you defend as is your right,
Prepare to walk into the night,
A shadow thing without regret,
Someone to mourn perchance forget;
You choose to do what you decide,
And in the sky the angels cried.

Alistair Muir 2016

Harvest Moon

The bloodshed rife this harvest moon,
Where every schizo, madman, loon,
Throws back his head, emits a howl,
Wears on his face an evil scowl;
And ventures forth to rent and kill,
A deadly art, a practised skill,
But more than that the great desire,
Perverse, macabre, an inner fire;

So many deaths this autumn night,
The blood glints in the orange light,
Eviscerated organs lie,
Upon the road and to the eye,
Appear as art, the madmen smile,
To thus create is to defile.

Alistair Muir 2016

114

Summer Comes

The summer comes to grace the land
Yet still we strain to understand
For Nature sings an air of need
Yet Man hears not because of greed;
Sweet Gaia cries her tears of pain
To nurture flora with her rain,

The trees respond and branches sway
And in the wind hear what they say;
Strange sibilants an eery sound,
Recrimination does resound,
A plague on Man for errant deeds
Recouping more than what He needs,

We stand and watch the Earth abused,
Grow so non-plussed and yet confused
As climate change destroys the air,
We act as if we do not care;
So now the summer comes to us,
Presents a show so glorious,

The nascent buds and fauna's young
To mothers' bosom tightly clung,
The growth abounds yet still we err,
Such negligence beyond compare;
We rape the Earth and barren leave,
So fatuous we can't believe

The things we do are so unkind,
We wander round as if we're blind;
'Tis now the time to make amends
And emulate the tribe that tends
The fertile ground, embraces Earth,
Avoids the hardship and the dearth;

So listen to the trees my friend,
They try to teach and not offend.

Mental Camp-Out

And so you drift into your world,
Just like a nascent infant curled,
Upon enchanted forest floor
A fantasy, an open door
To lands that time and space forgot,
Idyllic scene a perfect spot;

Then unicorns so wild and free
Appear to charm your reverie,
So pure and white, such innocence,
No mask, disguise or fake pretence;
For they are safe here in your mind,
No predators herein confined;

You camp out in the forest glade,
The ancient trees providing shade,
And for a while this fantasy
Supplants your sad reality,
The day to day dissolves in peace
A merciful and swift release.

Alistair Muir 2016

Down and Out

So down and out the fool lays down
And flickers cross his face a frown,
He digs a hand in pocket deep
The emptiness moves him to weep;
Sad tears of such frustration, ire,
With hunger burning like a fire,
A need to feed on drugs and drink
To hide away and not to think;
For life is nasty, brutish, short,
And in a downward spiral caught
Addiction reigns, the ship off course,
Unable to return to source;

The tiredness comes, a fitful sleep,
As into his environs creep
The vagabonds or ne'er-do-well
Who lie and steal and bodies sell;
They search around upon him spit
He tries to move, attempts to sit,
And then a thing incredible,
If told would deem it risible;
She now descends from who knows where,
Perchance a Goddess, silver hair
Falls down around her perfect form,
Her eyes were oval, huge and warm;

And does she now extend a palm
Her sweet demeanour fosters calm,
Though hesitant he takes the hand
She bids him rise and so does stand;
An intervention from on high
The motivation to stay dry,
Now passes from the girl to he
Who doubts his own warped sanity;
And then she disappears from view
And leaves the man with much to rue,
His errant past now hence to change
And future times to re-arrange.

Stabbed

And so you stab him your old friend,
Deep in the heart but you pretend
That it is you who bleeds in pain,
Not he who stares with such disdain;
So envious of him you are,
Have always been and will be far
Into the future, mark my word,
Though it may sound perverse, absurd;
And he who bleeds what of his need?
Do you deny him succour, feed?
Abandoned in his hour of hope
Attacked because you could not cope
With jealousy, how sad this end
Between a victim and his friend.

Alistair Muir 2016

Gifted?

They say he's gifted, chosen, rare,
But this is falsehood, just hot air,
For sinister the mind of he
Engaged in such affrontery;
He dazzles eyes with magic tricks,
His peer group laughs and bottom licks,
So confident at ease at play,
His secret shuns the light of day;

For come the night, the witching hour,
The source of his fantastic power,
On bended knee he genuflects,
Prays to the One he loves, respects;
Beelzebub the prince of lies,
To him the source of all that's wise,
Now trades his soul for sleight of hand
'Tis difficult to understand

The rights and wrongs but he has made
His final choice, not he dismayed
That he will spend eternity,
A thrall of evil entity;
For now we stand applaud the fool
His magic tricks which look so cool,
And he begins the slide to hell,
We fear for him but wish him well.

Alistair Muir 2016

119

Summer Days

And so you sit and rest the mind,
Unto the past are you consigned
On wings of thought you fly to when
The Earth was cool and in was Zen;
Those hippy days of love and peace
The tie-dye shirts, a sheepskin fleece,

When drugs were hip and everywhere,
A mental trip to who knows where,
The grass was toked and acid dropped
And no-one wanted smoking stopped;
The mind expansion was a ride
So smooth a run, electra glide;

As kids we knew of nothing wrong,
Apart from Woody, protest song,
The marches for our Civil Rights
Along with racist bigots, fights;
For we were blissful, ignorant,
Too young to join the global chant

No life was good those summers long,
We were at peace our friendships strong
And most of all were they still here,
Your mother, father, sister dear;
Now long gone it is good to look
Way back and open up your book.

Alistair Muir 2016

Utopian Dreams

And in all truth you crave the peace,
Utopia, a sweet release
From global dearth and civil war
The trappings of the trophy whore;
What is needed is a gift,
 Something so huge to cause a shift,
A way to balance, care, respect,
The lack of which you see, detect
In everyday activity,
Such social ambiguity
And nastiness, for we are caught
In lives so nasty, brutish, short;
Perchance a miracle or two
Will grant a peace for me and you.

Alistair Muir 2016

My Princess

Not often now you pen this kind of verse
Refreshing is the flow of verb and noun
So easy to recant and not perverse
You strive to pen an ode of some renown;
A theme for this be love and surely she
The author of your peace and tranquil mind
Will fill the page with wit and constancy
The like of which is difficult to find;
For she a goddess is your constant muse
And graces with her beauty every page
Her presence serves to heighten and bemuse
She is the very light by which you guage
Your happiness and all there is in joy
The princess and the ever-youthful boy.

Alistair Muir 2016

Just Say No

And so it was back in the day
The drugs were rife, what can you say?
A smoke of green a tab or two,
Perhaps some coke or something new;
You dabbled did experiment
Along with peers, was surely meant,
No damage done to mind or brain
These substances you now abstain;

But that was then but here today
The drugs work in a different way,
So pure the skunk, the THC
Like crystals you can easy see;
But strong and lethal is this weed
Which forms addiction from its need,
And from the grass is short a stride
To climb on board the Class A ride;

You look around and you can see
The H abusers easily,
Their eyes are dead as is their hope
Now sliding down the slippery slope;
Addiction's child so keen to please,
Now move on to the classy E's
And watch in shame your A and E
Fill to the roof dramatically;

Detritus of a human kind,
The flotsam, jetsom of Mankind
This isn't how it should have been
It's only weed, a little green,
But kids today are fooled by peers,
To turn drugs down means facing jeers
And reprimands, you must comply
A reason that so many die;

Too strong too fast must we beware
Or else our own will simply dare
And there will come a time one night,
When cops arrive to give a fright;
Another victim of this shit
An E, or H or composite,
And you will lose another son,
A young life lost before begun.

Alistair Muir 2016

Love Sonnet

And so you sit and empty out your heart
To she your muse who now attends your hand
Such sad confession now does love impart
A fact sweet Terpsichore does understand;
For you are so in love it shines from eyes
Grown weary now but still reflecting joy
You try to write before the lovelight dies
And 'fore the morning comes to wake, destroy
The inspiration to effect a verse,
A piece that will excite, entice, inure
This ode you read and must in truth rehearse
To prove to her your love is real and pure;
So come the spirits to watch over you,
To bolster faded pride and here imbue.

Alistair Muir 2016

Thought Police

And so appear the thought police,
Who here attempt to keep the peace
Already bound the female cries
Her simple thought of love decries;
But no, too late, the thought is out,
For them a whisper is a shout
So sinister in dress and form
In helmets and black uniform;
Betrayed the female's mind is read
Better for her if she was dead
For now begins retraining, pain,
Invasive, drives one quite insane;
Beware all thoughts of love, release,
For freedom summons thought police.

Alistair Muir 2016

Leadership Election 2016

In Britain do we face more choice
A chance to pick our leading voice,
Could it be fair Theresa May
Or will Andrea spoil the day?
With liberty, democracy
We shun complete autocracy,
Our government doth need a lead
Now candidates of us do plead
Our little X upon the slip,
To find the captain of the ship;
But should we not election hold?
All parties in forever bold
Perchance but first the leader pick
Replace the former yellow prick.

Alistair Muir 2016

126

The Eternal Optimist

You view the world a half full glass,
An optimist who trusts to fate
But should things turn and kick your arse
You're evermore still obdurate;
What is the point of constant doubt
Or thinking that the world will end?
No better to endure a clout
About the head from good a friend;
To emphasise the positive
Is clearly now the thing to do
For thinking life so negative
Invites that end to thus ensue;
So concentrate on CBT
And live a life of quality.

Alistair Muir 2016

Cancer

And does disease now call to you
It terrorises, runs right through
Your system cells, immunity
Now just so much futility;
The pain exuded makes you weep,
Destroys your day, prevents all sleep
But still you think of life with hope
A necessary means to cope;
Tomorrow should it come at all
Will be a celebration ball,
Another deadline beaten, won,
Your re-birth only just begun;
No life is hard but sweet and chaste,
You long tomorrow now with haste.

Alistair Muir 2016

Exit Stage Right

And so you exit now stage right
To disappear into the night
A lonely figure mask adorned,
Forever cursed and inward scorned;
Your destination has been set
For you a sense of fear, regret
As wasted has your life been here
Too many drugs washed down with beer;
Inferno waits for such as you,
A wastrel drunk without a clue
Who trod the boards now waits in shame
With only you yourself to blame;
So enter hell and medicine take,
Your time on Earth you must foresake.

Alistair Muir 2016

She Weeps

Dream on and watch the tears fall from her eyes
Sweet Gaia weeps for Man and planet Earth
The rain descends from blue and purple skies
But 'tis too late the land condemned to dearth;
For Man has here abused and raped the land
His greed doth know no bounds for He is free
Unchained yet still he fails to understand
The price of his continued liberty;
She watches as defiled her fauna die
The savage beast to blame for Gaia's pain
In faeces and detritus children cry
For pestilence accompanies the rain;
With war and famine rife She prays for peace
But knows inside the torment will increase.

Alistair Muir 2016

Joyous Love

And joy does here abound my heart is full
To hear her voice sends shivers down my spine
And to its charm I feel a constant pull
That of a love that's great I would opine;
A glance from azure eyes and I am there
Mere puppet in her hands I am compleat
And should a tender kiss I choose to dare
Feel confident I meet with no defeat;
For she is mine and I a lucky man
To have the trust of such an angel fair
I feel as winner not an also-ran
To be with such as she beyond compare;
So kneel I now in supplication Lord
For peace and love which only you afford.

Alistair Muir 2016

Printed in Great Britain
by Amazon